Pebble® Plus

LET'S LOOK AT COUNTRIES

LET'S LOOK AT

# SOUTH AFRICA

NIKKI BRUNO CLAPPER

raintree

a Capstone company — publishers for children

Raintree is an imprint of Capstone Global Library Limited, a company incorporated in England and Wales having its registered office at 264 Banbury Road, Oxford, OX2 7DY – Registered company number: 6695582

www.raintree.co.uk
myorders@raintree.co.uk

Edited by Carrie Sheely
Designed by Juliette Peters
Picture research by Tracy Cummins
Production by Laura Manthe
Originated by Capstone Global Library Limited
Printed and bound in India

ISBN 978 1 4747 5306 7
22 21 20 19 18
10 9 8 7 6 5 4 3 2 1

**British Library Cataloguing in Publication Data**
A full catalogue record for this book is available from the British Library.

**Acknowledgements**
We would like to thank the following for permission to reproduce photographs: Getty Images: Francois Nel, 16; iStockphoto: Henrique NDR Martins, 13, ManoAfrica, 1; Shutterstock: Andrea Willmore, 22–23, 24, bonchan, 19, Denis Mironov, 21, elleon, 9, Francesco Dazzi, 5, Garth Fuchs, Cover Top, Globe Turner, 22 Top, Hedrus, 11, JMx Images, 10, Linda Nienaber, Cover Bottom, Cover Back, Mai Groves, 17, Monkey Business Images, 15, nale, 4, Olaf Holland, 3, Richard van der Spuy, 6–7, Utopia_88, Cover Middle

Every effort has been made to contact copyright holders of material reproduced in this book. Any omissions will be rectified in subsequent printings if notice is given to the publisher.

All the internet addresses (URLs) given in this book were valid at the time of going to press. However, due to the dynamic nature of the internet, some addresses may have changed, or sites may have changed or ceased to exist since publication. While the author and publisher regret any inconvenience this may cause readers, no responsibility for any such changes can be accepted by either the author or the publisher.

# CONTENTS

# Where is South Africa?

South Africa is a country
at the southern tip of Africa.
Its capitals are Pretoria,
Cape Town and Bloemfontein.

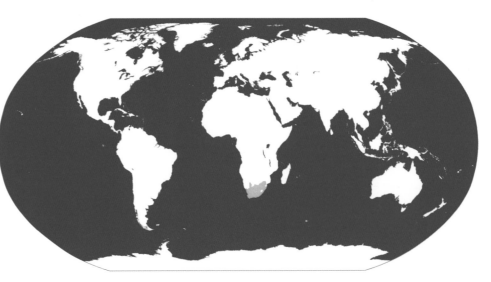

■ South Africa

## From grasslands to mountains

Much of South Africa's land is a plateau covered in grasslands. The climate is dry. Droughts are common.

Mountain ranges surround
the grasslands in a U shape.
The most famous range
is called the Drakensberg.
This means "Dragon's Mountain."

# In the wild

Leopards, cheetahs and lions live in the grasslands. They hunt zebras, wildebeest and antelope. Penguins live along the coast.

lion

zebras

# People

South Africa's people have

many different backgrounds.

Many people are black.

Others are white, Asian

or mixed race.

# At work

Some South Africans

work in gold mines.

Others build cars or

make clothes in factories.

Jobs in tourism are common.

# On the field

Many South Africans love sports. Rugby, boxing and running are popular. Athletes climb, cycle and hike in the mountains.

rugby

# At the table

South Africans eat a lot of meat. The meat is often barbecued or dried. Bobotie is baked meat mixed with egg and fruit.

bobotie

# A famous site

Table Mountain towers

over the city of Cape Town.

The mountain has a flat top.

People climb it on foot or

visit it in a cable car.

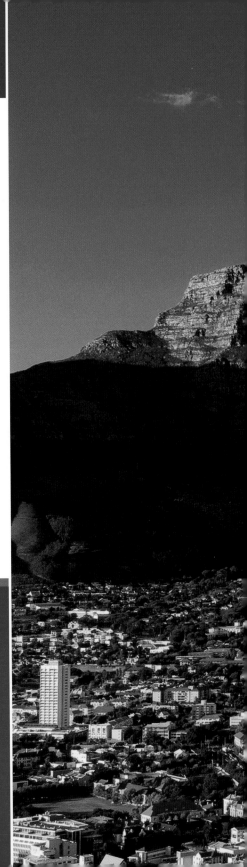

# QUICK SOUTH AFRICA FACTS

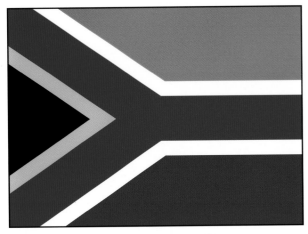
South African flag

**Name:** Republic of South Africa

**Capitals:** Pretoria, Cape Town, Bloemfontein

**Other major cities:** Johannesburg, Durban

**Population:** 54,300,704 (July 2016 estimate)

**Size:** 1,219,090 square km (470,693 sq mi)

**Languages:** isiZulu, isiXhosa, Afrikaans, English, isiNdebele, SeSotho, Sesotho sa Leboa, SiSwati, Xitsonga, Setswana, Tshivenda

**Money:** rand

# GLOSSARY

**background** information that helps describe a person, such as race, education level and religion

**cable car** car pulled by an overhead or underground cable

**capital** city in a country where the government is based

**climate** average weather of a place throughout the year

**drought** when the land is dry because of too little rain

**mine** place where workers dig up minerals that are underground

**plateau** area of high, flat land

**tourism** business of taking care of visitors to a country or place

# FIND OUT MORE

## BOOKS

*Cultural Traditions in South Africa* (Cultural Traditions in My World), Molly Aloian (Crabtree, 2014)

*Living in . . . South Africa.* (Living in . . .), Chloe Perkins (Simon Spotlight, 2016)

*South Africa,* Kate Shoup (Cavendish Square Publishing, 2018)

## WEBSITES

https://www.activityvillage.co.uk/south-africa
Discover activities and facts about South Africa!

https://www.tenfactsabout.co.uk/0024rugby.htm
Learn more about rugby, South Africa's popular sport.

http://www.bbc.co.uk/nature/places/Africa
Find out about Africa's wildlife.

# COMPREHENSION QUESTIONS

1. Name some sports and activities South Africans enjoy?

2. What is a capital?

3. How can people get to the top of Table Mountain?

# INDEX